ENUMA ELISH

Vol. II

Luzac's

Semitic Text and Translation Series.

Vol. XIII

AMS PRESS
NEW YORK

Part of the Third Tablet of the Creation Series (Brit. Mus., No. 93,017).

THE SEVEN TABLETS

OF

CREATION,

OR THE BABYLONIAN AND ASSYRIAN LEGENDS
CONCERNING THE CREATION OF THE WORLD
AND OF MANKIND.

EDITED BY

L. W. KING, M.A., F.S.A.,

ASSISTANT IN THE DEPARTMENT OF EGYPTIAN AND ASSYRIAN ANTIQUITIES, BRITISH MUSEUM.

VOL. II.

SUPPLEMENTARY TEXTS.

London :
LUZAC AND CO.
1902.

Library of Congress Cataloging in Publication Data

Enuma elish.
    The seven tablets of creation.

    Reprint of the 1902 ed. published by Luzac and
Co., London, which was issued as v. 12-13 of Luzac's
Semitic text and translation series.
    Includes indexes.
    CONTENTS: v. 1. English translations, etc.—v. 2.
Supplementary texts.
    1. Creation. 2. Cosmogony, Babylonian. 3. Assyro-
Babylonian language—Texts. I. King, Leonard William,
1869-1919. II. Title.
PJ3771.E5   1976   892'.1   73-18850
ISBN 0-404-11344-3

Reprinted with permission from a volume in the
Library of Bryn Mawr College, 1976

From the edition of 1902, London
First AMS edition published in 1976
Manufactured in the United States of America

International Standard Book Number:
Complete Set: 0-404-11344-3
Volume II: 0-404-11346-X

AMS PRESS INC.
NEW YORK, N. Y. 10003

Preface.

In this volume is published for the first time the texts from a group of tablets, inscribed in the Neo-Babylonian character, and containing new portions of the great series of Creation Legends, to which the Assyrians and Babylonians gave the title *Enuma elish.* The group includes :—1. Portions of four copies of the First Tablet of the series, together with two extracts from the text, inscribed upon rough "practice-tablets" by the pupils of Babylonian scribes ; 2. Portions of two copies of the Second Tablet of the series ; 3. Part of a copy of the Third Tablet, and fragments of three "practice-tablets" inscribed with portions of the text, which I have joined to other similar fragments already published in *Cuneiform Texts from Babylonian Tablets, etc., in the British Museum*, Part XIII (1901) ; 4. Part of a copy of the Sixth Tablet, which is of peculiar interest inasmuch as it refers to the Creation of Man, and settles the disputed question as to the number of Tablets, or sections, of which the Creation Series was composed ; and 5. Portions of two copies of the Seventh Tablet of the series.

A "practice-tablet," which is inscribed in the Sumerian and Babylonian languages with texts relating to the Creation of the Moon and of the Sun, is also included.

The Appendices contain texts which, for the most part, are closely connected with the interpretation of the Creation Legends. They include :—1. A number of Assyrian commentaries on the Seventh Tablet of the Creation Series, together with fragments of texts which are similar in character to that composition ; 2. A Neo-Babylonian duplicate of the tablet which has been supposed to belong to the Creation Series and to contain the instructions given to man after his creation, but which is now shown by the new duplicate to be part of a tablet of moral precepts and to have no connection whatsoever with the Creation Series ; 3. Part of a large astrological text of the period of the Arsacidae, in which some of the chief personages of the Creation-story appear in astrological characters, and the story itself is interpreted on astrological lines ; and 4. The text of the legend which was at one time commonly, but erroneously, believed to contain an Assryian version of the story of the Tower of Babel. The last appendix contains a " Prayer of the Raising of the Hand to Ishtar," which belongs to the series of similar compositions already published in my *Babylonian Magic and Sorcery* (1896); both from the beauty of its language and from its perfect state of preservation, it must be regarded as one of the finest and most complete Babylonian religious texts which have hitherto been recovered.

After the plates in this volume had been printed off, and whilst I was engaged in making a hand-list of the smaller fragments in the Kuyunjik Collections, I identified ten additional fragments of the Creation Series, belonging to copies of the First, Second, Fifth, and Seventh Tablets of the composition. The texts of these fragments, as well as those of some other closely allied Assyrian and Neo-Babylonian tablets, are published by means of outline blocks in the first volume of this work.

L. W. KING.

LONDON, July 29th, 1902.

Contents.

Supplementary Texts.

45528 + 46614.

OBVERSE.

45528 + 46614.

OBVERSE (Cont.).

45528 + 46614.

OBVERSE (Cont.).

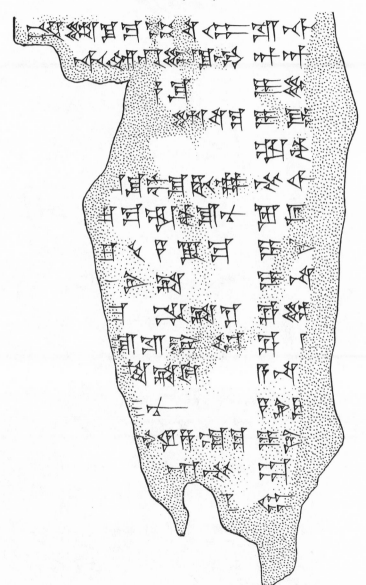

45528 + 46614.

REVERSE.

45528 + 46614.

REVERSE (Cont.).

45528 + 46614.

REVERSE (Cont.).

35134.

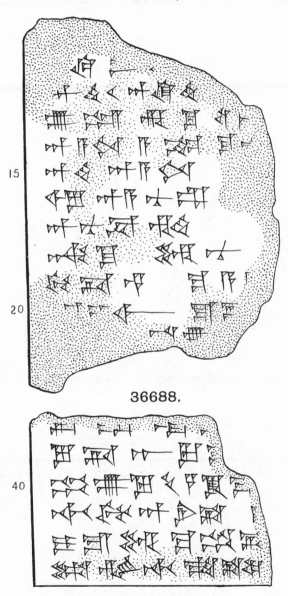

36688.

The text is an extract from a
practice-tablet.

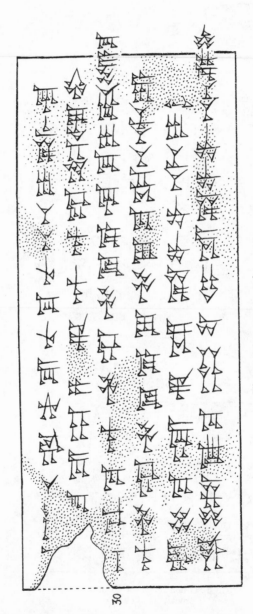

36726.

The text is an extract from a practice-tablet.

30

46803.

OBVERSE.

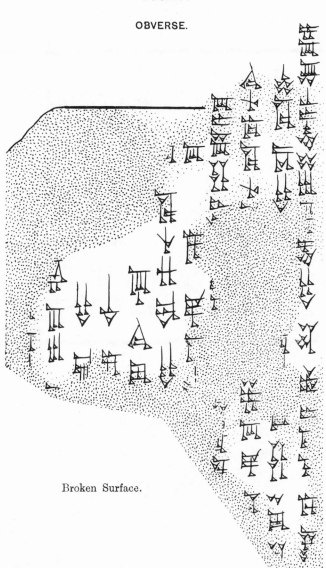

Broken Surface.

46803.

OBVERSE (cont.) & REVERSE

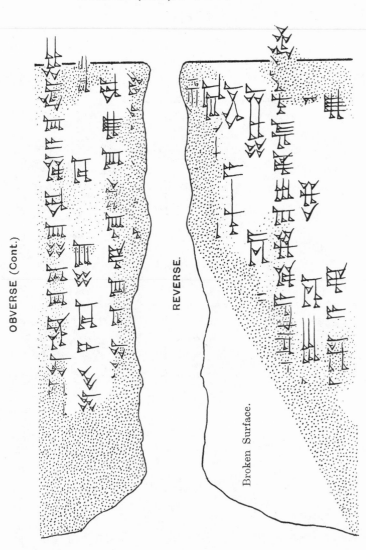

46803.

REVERSE (cont.).

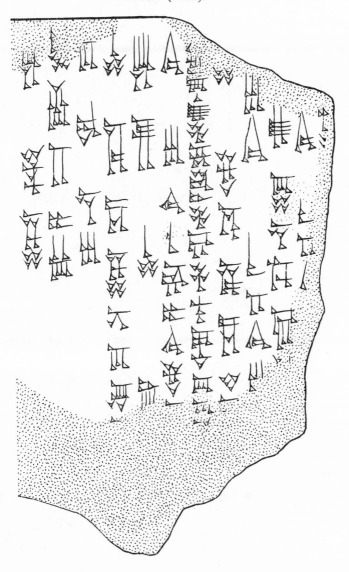

82-9-18, 6879.

REVERSE.

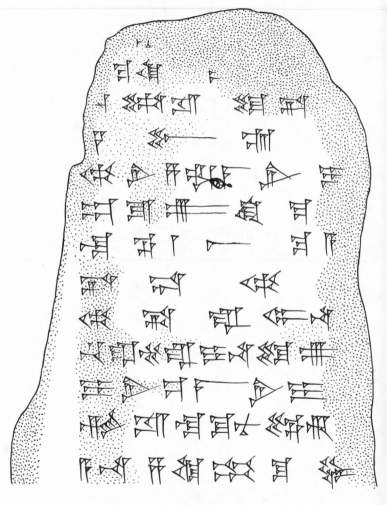

The Obverse of the fragment
is missing.

82-9-18, 6879.

REVERSE (cont.).

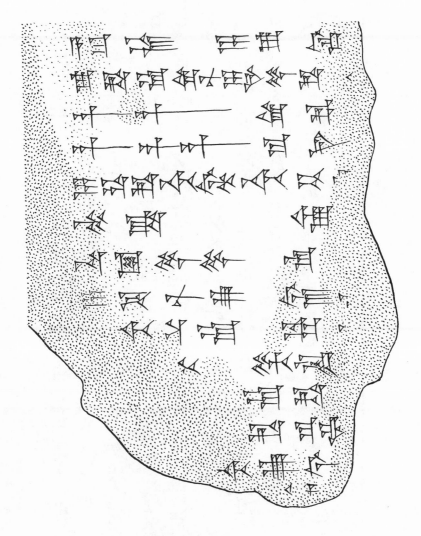

40559.

OBVERSE.

40559.

OBVERSE (cont.).

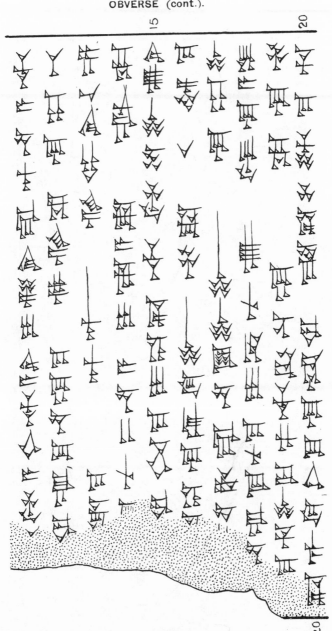

40559.

OBVERSE (cont.).

40559.

OBVERSE (cont.).

40559.

REVERSE.

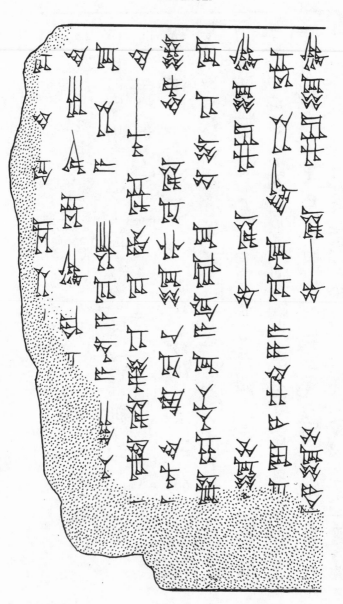

40559.

REVERSE (cont.).

40559.

REVERSE (Cont.).

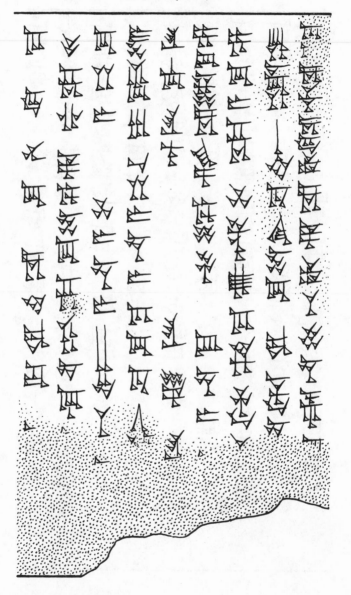

40559.

REVERSE (cont.).

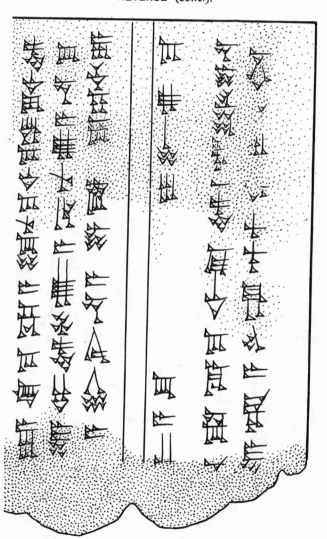

92632 + 93048.

OBVERSE.

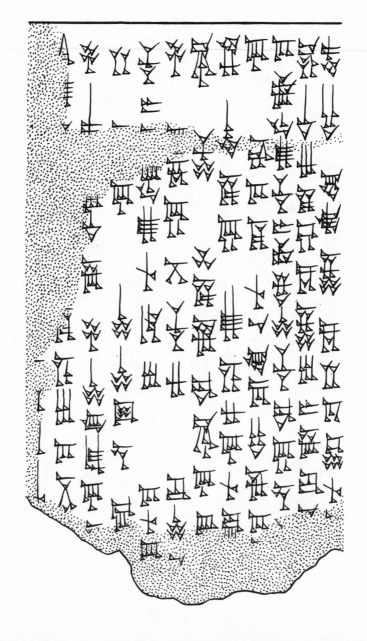

92632 + 93048.

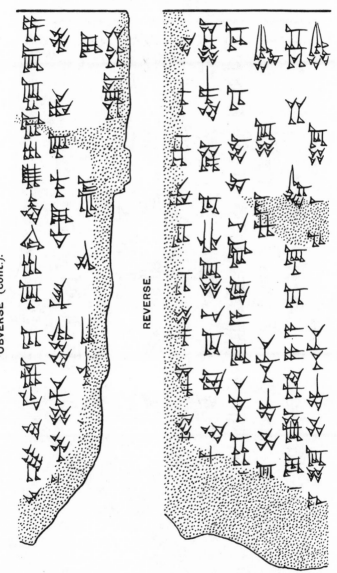

OBVERSE (cont.).

REVERSE.

92632 + 93048.

REVERSE (cont.).

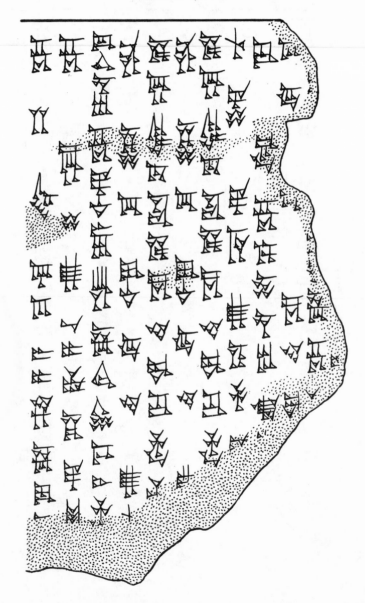

82-9-18, 1403 + 6316.

OBVERSE.

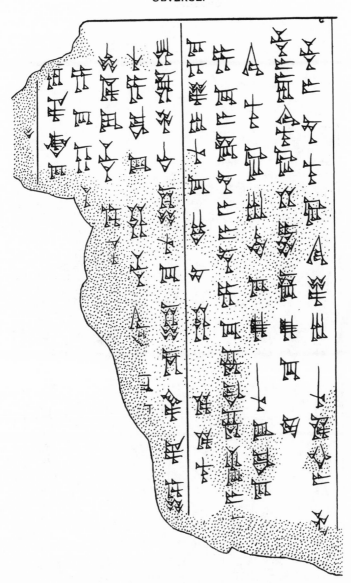

82-9-18, 1403 + 6316.

OBVERSE (Cont.).

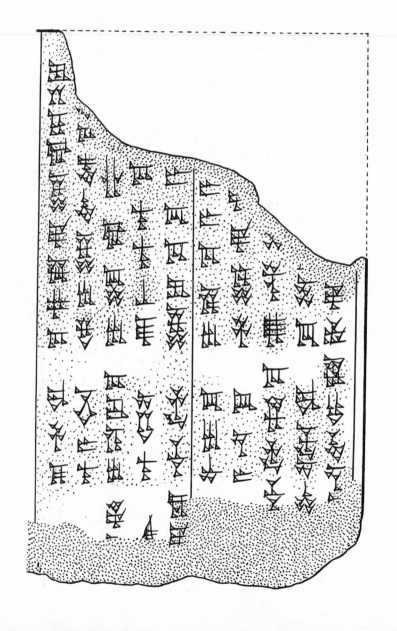

82-9-18, 1403 + 6316.

REVERSE.

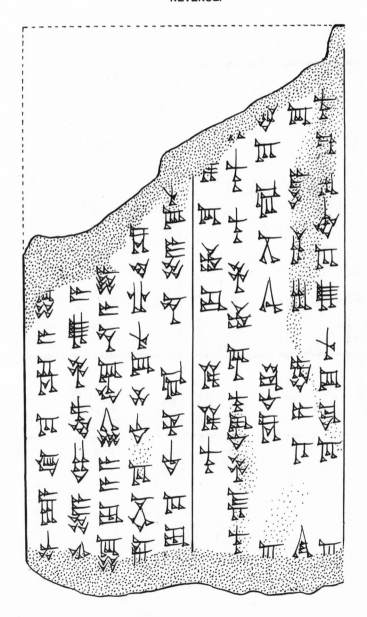

82-9-18, 1403 + 6316.

REVERSE (Cont.).

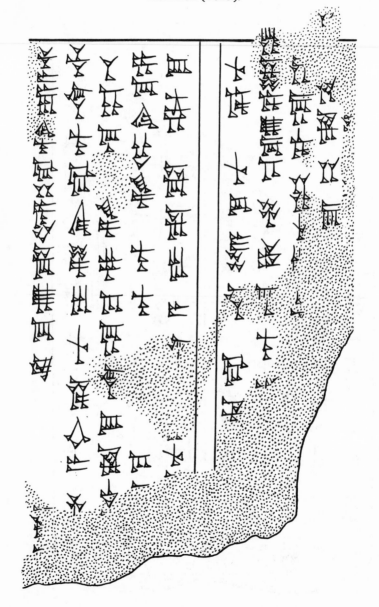

82-9-18, 6950 + 83-1-18, 1868.

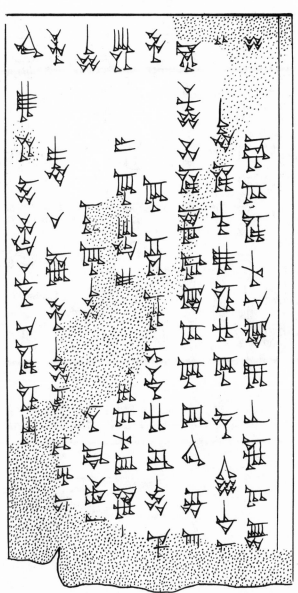

The text is an extract from a
practice-tablet.

42285.

OBVERSE.

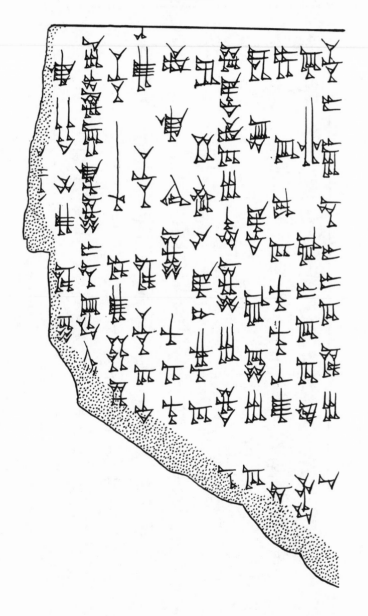

42285.

OBVERSE (Cont.).

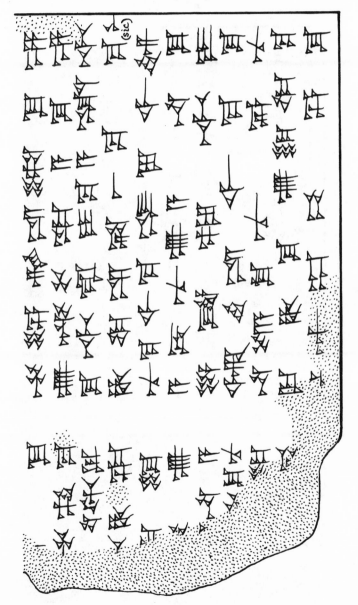

42285.

REVERSE.

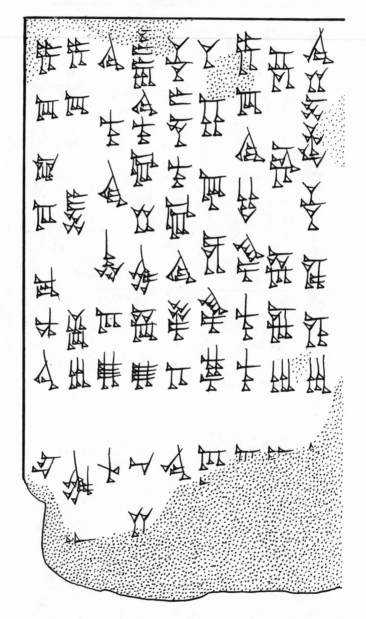

42285.

REVERSE (Cont.).

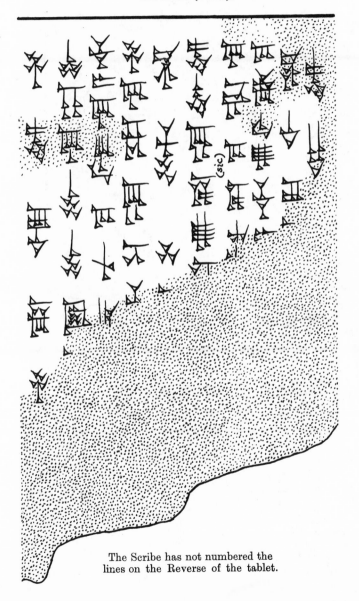

The Scribe has not numbered the
lines on the Reverse of the tablet.

82-9-18, 5448   +   83-1-18, 2116.

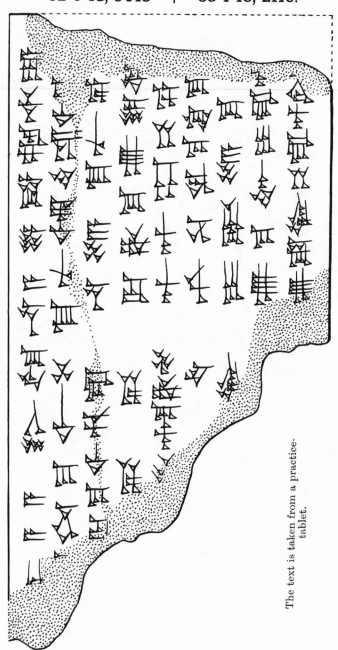

The text is taken from a practice-tablet.

92629.

OBVERSE.

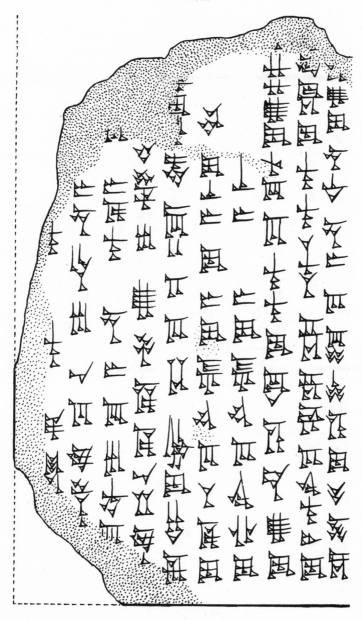

92629.

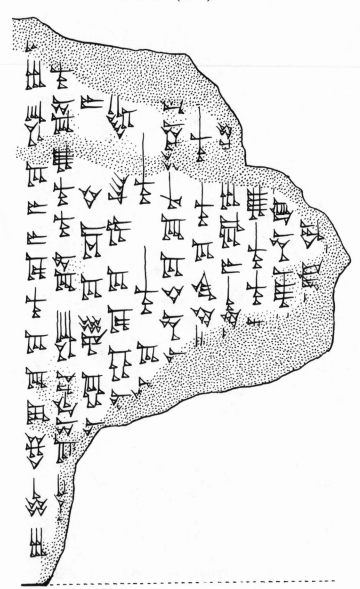

92629.

REVERSE.

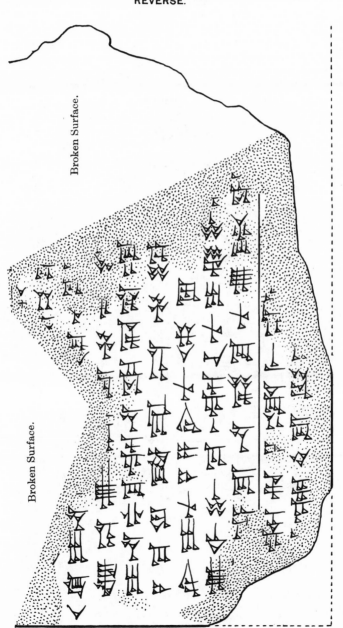

91139 + 93073.

OBVERSE.

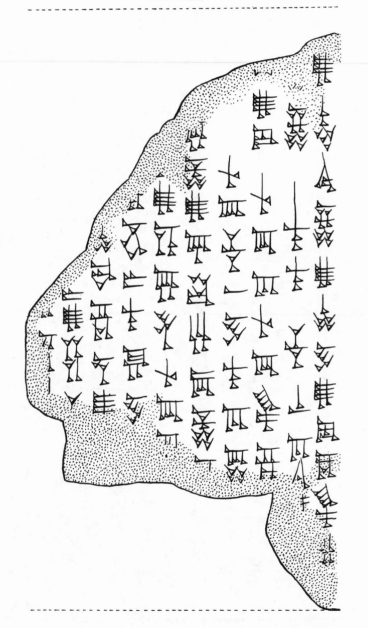

91139 + 93073.

OBVERSE (cont.).

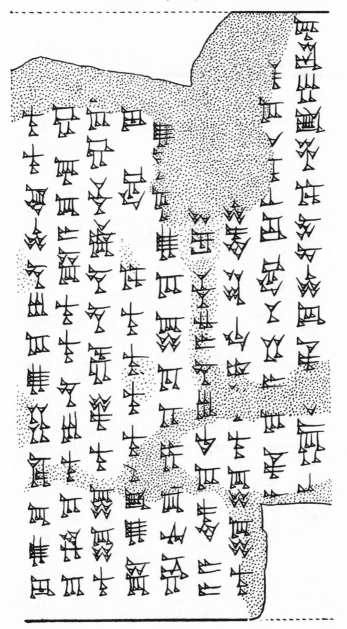

91139 + 93073.

OBVERSE (cont.).

OBVERSE (Cont.).

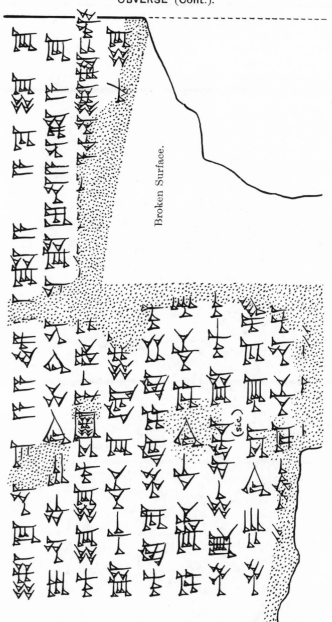

91139 + 93073.

REVERSE (cont.).

1. Erasure by the Scribe.

91139 + 93073.

REVERSE (cont.).

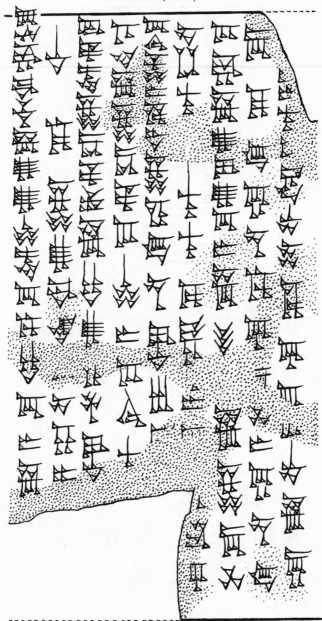

91139 + 93073.

REVERSE (cont.).

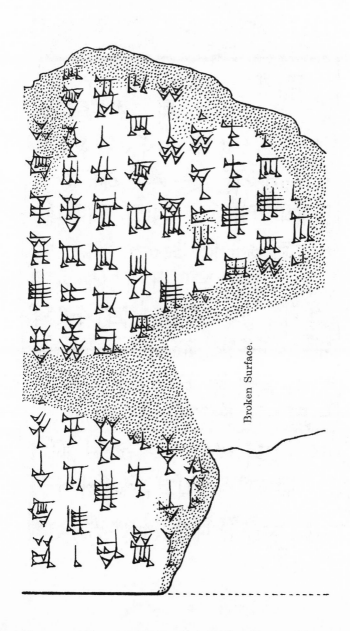

Broken Surface.

35506.

OBVERSE.

35506.

OBVERSE (Cont.).

REVERSE.

35506.

REVERSE (Cont.).

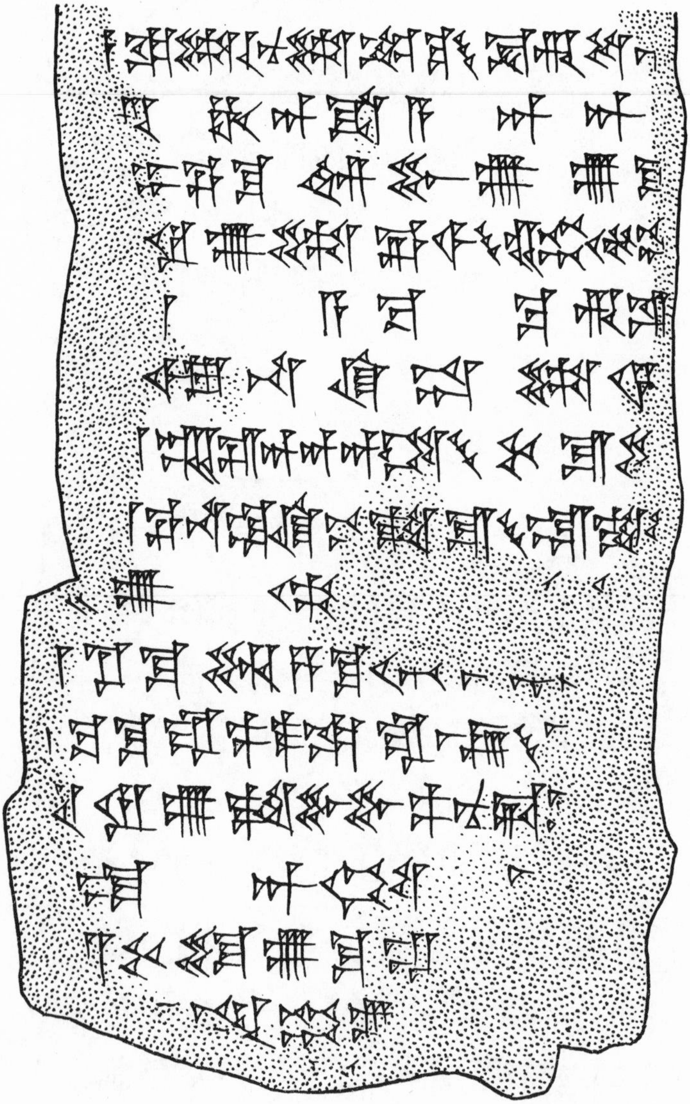

82-7-14, 4005.

OBVERSE.

82-7-14, 4005.

REVERSE

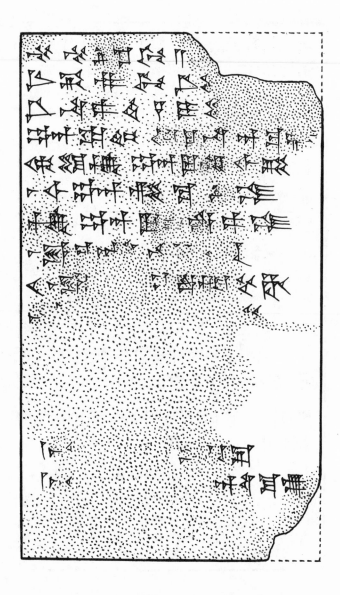

S. 11 + S. 980.

OBVERSE.

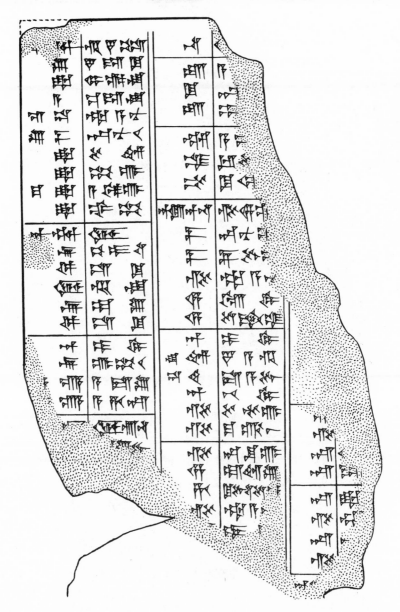

S. 11 + S. 980.

REVERSE.

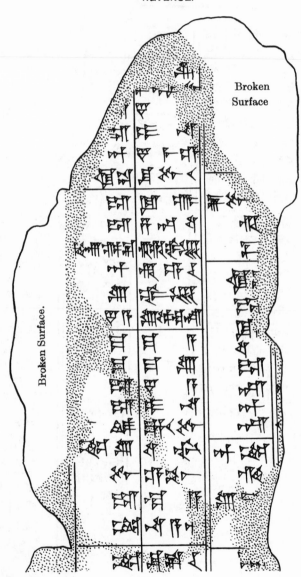

Broken
Surface

Broken Surface.

S. 11 + S. 980.

REVERSE (Cont.).

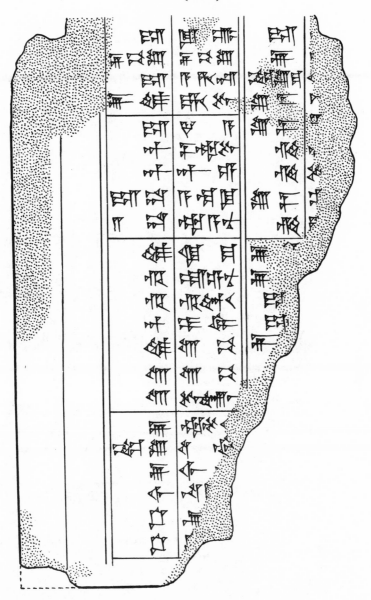

K. 4406.

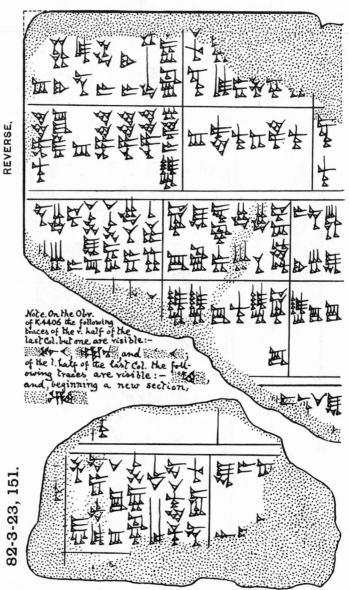

Note. On the Obv.
of K 4406 the following
traces of the r. half of the
last Col. but one are visible:—
〈traces〉 and 〈traces〉
of the l. half of the last Col. the following traces are visible:— 〈trace〉,
and, beginning a new section,
〈trace〉

K. 4406.

REVERSE (Cont.).

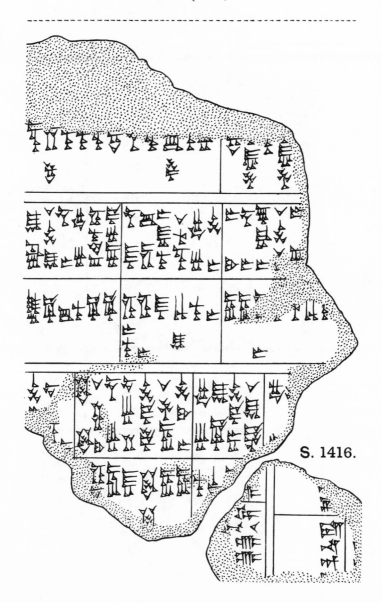

S. 1416.

R. 366 + 80-7-19, 293.

OBVERSE.

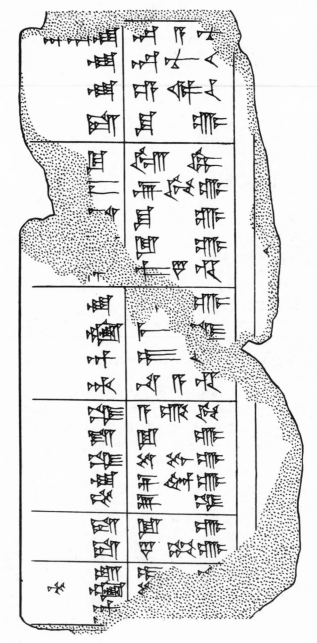

R. 366 + 80-7-19, 293.

REVERSE.

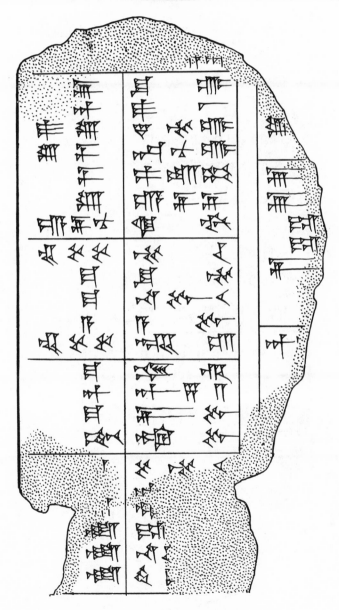

R. 366 + 80-7-19, 293.

REVERSE (cont.).

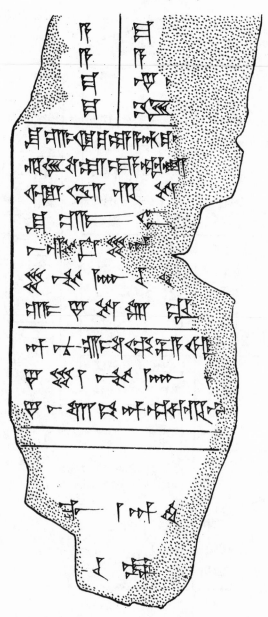

K. 2053.

OBVERSE.

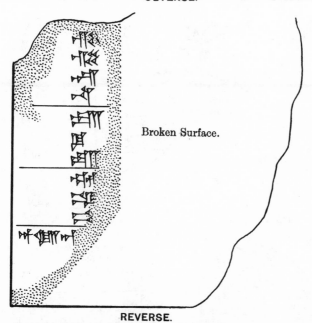

Broken Surface.

REVERSE.

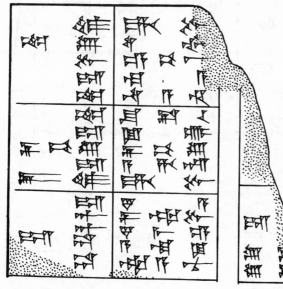

K. 2053.

REVERSE (cont.).

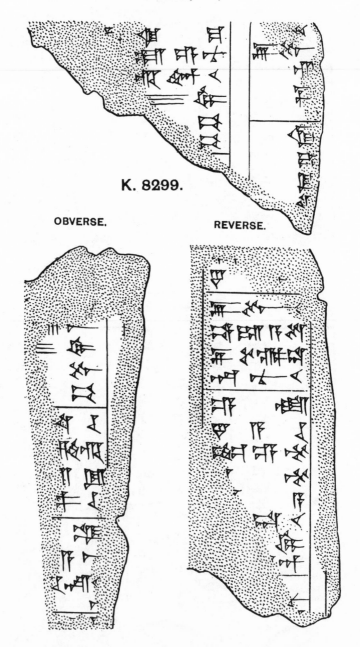

K. 8299.

OBVERSE.   REVERSE.

K. 2107 + K. 6086.

OBVERSE.

The Reverse of the Tablet is inscribed
with a list of Temples.

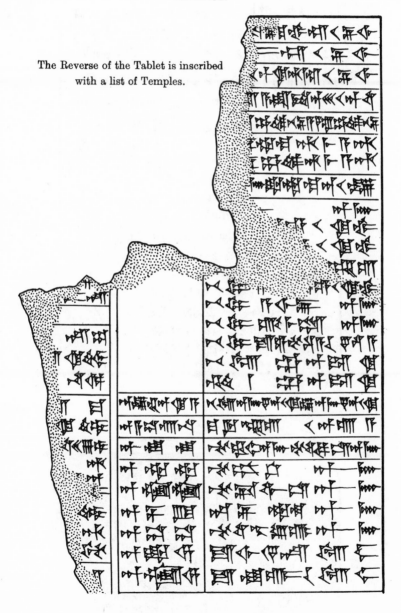

K. 2107 + K. 6086.

OBVERSE (Cont.).

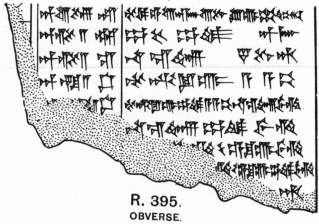

R. 395.
OBVERSE.

REVERSE.

54228.

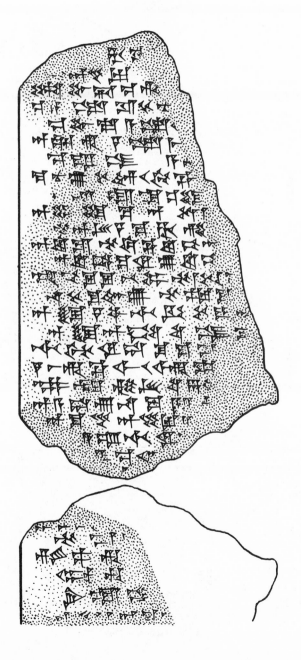

33851.

OBVERSE.

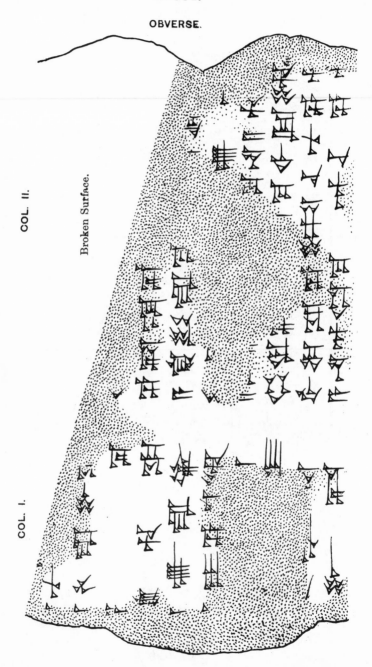

COL. II.

Broken Surface.

COL. I.

33851.

OBVERSE (Cont.).

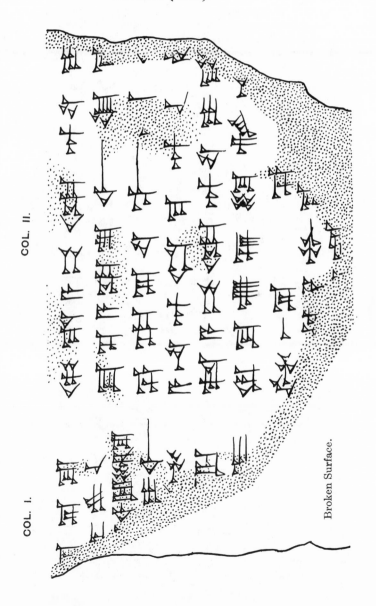

COL. II.

COL. I.

Broken Surface.

33851.

REVERSE.

COL. III.

COL. IV.

55466+55486+55627.

OBVERSE.

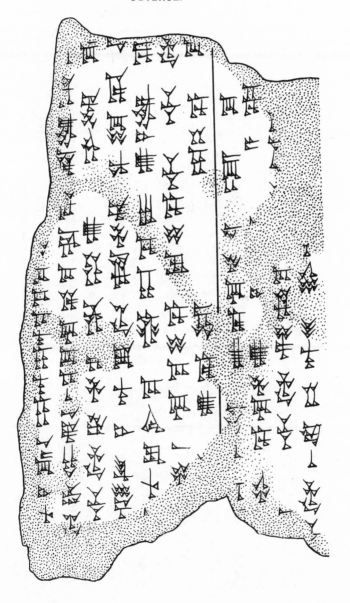

55466+55486+55627.

OBVERSE (Cont.).

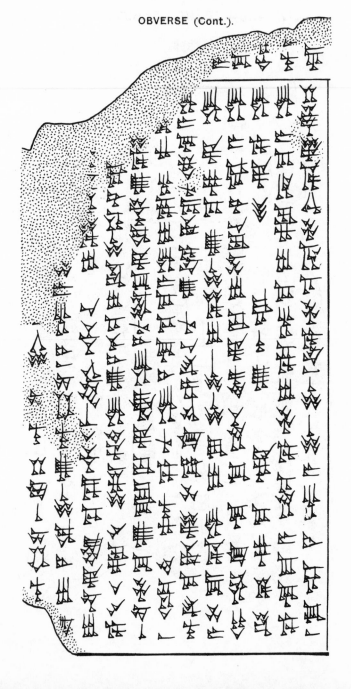

55466+55486+55627.

OBVERSE. (Cont.).

55466+55486+55627.

REVERSE.

55466+55486+55627.

REVERSE (Cont.).

55466+55486+55627.

REVERSE (Cont.).

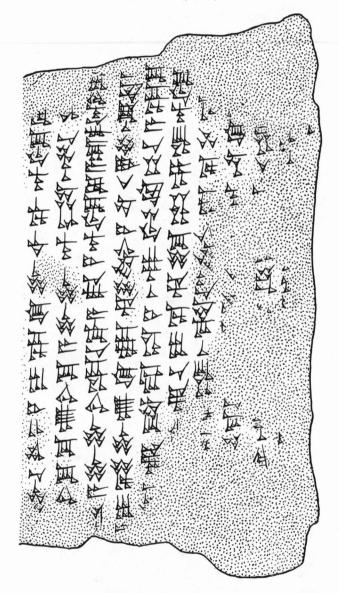

K. 3657.

OBVERSE.

Broken Surface.

K. 3657.

REVERSE.

26187.

OBVERSE

OBVERSE (cont.).

26187.

OBVERSE (Cont.).

erasure

26187.

OBVERSE (cont.).

26187.

OBVERSE (cont.).

50

55

50

55

1. One sign erased by the scribe.

26187.

REVERSE.

26187.

REVERSE (Cont.).

26187.

REVERSE (Cont.).

26187.

REVERSE (Cont.).

1. The second half of the line has been deeply erased by the Scribe.

26187.

REVERSE (Cont.).

Index to Plates.

Index to Plates—*continued*.